THE ULTIMATE WOOD PELLET SMOKER AND GRILL COOKBOOK

Delicious and Easy Step-by-Step BBQ Recipes for Beginners and Advanced Pitmasters

2nd Edition

Pitmaster Academy

Table of Content

INTRODUCTION

Pellet grills are revolutionary and may forever change the way we cook. Modern pellet grills make cooking enjoyable and hassle-free.

It also eliminates guesswork thanks to the easy-to-follow recipes and the ability to remotely monitor and adjust your temperatures. Whether you're an amateur home cook hosting a backyard cookout or a pitmaster at a barbecue competition, a wood pellet grill can easily become one of the most important appliances you can own to help you make flavorful meals with much less effort.

Whether you love smoking, grilling, roasting, barbecuing, or direct cooking of food, a wood pellet grill is clearly versatile and has got you covered.

Cooking with a wood pellet grill allows you to choose the desired flavor of wood pellets to create the perfect smoke to flavor your food. Each wood pellet type has its personality and taste. The best part is you can use a single flavor or experiment to mix and match the flavors to invent your own combination.

Just like any cooking appliance, wood pellets have some drawbacks, but the benefits overshadow them. It is, therefore, definitely worth a try. These days, one popular method of cooking is smoking, which many enthusiasts use. Proteins such as meat, poultry and fish will be ruined quickly if modern cooking techniques are used. On the other hand, smoking is a process that takes a long time and low temperature, which thoroughly cooks the meat. The smoke, especially white smoke, greatly enhances the flavor of almost any food item. But more than that, smoking seals and preserves the nutrients in the food. Smoking is flexible and is one of the oldest techniques for making food.

Try cooking meat products for several hours using a heat source not directly on the meat. But you have to make sure that the smoke has a space to soak your meat and give it access way out

The picture of a good time with loved ones, neighbors and friends having a backyard barbeque is a pretty sight, isn't it? Having a smoker-grill and some grilled and smoked recipes are excellent when you have visitors at home. Because you can deliver both tasty food and a magical moment on a summer night, for example. Hundreds of fantastic recipes are available that you can try with a wood pellet smoker-grill! Experiment, improve, or make your own recipes – it is up to you. You can do it fast and easy. But if you want to be safe with the proven and tested ones, by all means, do so. These recipes have been known to be just right to the taste, and they work every time. A combination of creating a correct impression the first time and every time and enjoying tasty food along the way will be your edge.

Another great thing about these recipes is that they are easy to prepare and do not require you to be a wizard in the kitchen. By following a few easy steps and having the right ingredients at your disposal, you can use these recipes to make some delicious food in no time. So, try these recipes and spread the word! I'm sure this wood pellet smoker-grill recipe book will prove to be an invaluable gift to your loved ones, too!

Now you no longer have to scour the web, hunting for your favorite wood pellet smoker-grill recipes. This book is a one-stop solution designed to eliminate all your struggles in finding the perfect wood pellet smoker-grill recipes for yourself and your loved ones.

COOKING TIPS

Temperature and Times

With so many recipes to try with your pellet grill, it is easy to get overwhelmed right away. One important thing to keep in mind is that lower temperatures produce Smoke, while higher temperatures do not. Follow these useful tips below to know the temperature and time required to get the perfectly flavored meat each time.

- Beef briskets are best cooked at 250°F using the smoke setting for at least 4 hours by itself and covered with foil for another 4 hours.
- Pork ribs should be cooked at 275°F on the smoke setting for 3 hours and covered with foil for another 2-3 hours.
- Steaks require 400-450°F for about 10 minutes on each side.
- Turkey can be cooked at 375°F for 20 minutes per pound of meat. For smoked turkey, the heat settings should be around 180-225°F for 10-12 hours or until the turkeys inside reach 165°F.

- Chicken breasts can be cooked at 400-450°F for 15 minutes on each side.
- A whole chicken cooks at 400-450°F for 1.5 hours or until the internal temperature reaches 165°F.
- Bacon and Sausage can be cooked at 425°F for 5-8 minutes on each side.
- Hamburgers should be cooked at 350°F for at least 8 minutes for each side.
- You can smoke salmon for 1-1.5 hours and finish with a high setting for 2-3 minutes on each side.
- Shrimps cook at 400-450°F for 3-5 minutes on each side. If you prefer a smokier flavor, set the temperature at 225°F for about 30 minutes.

Cutting Types

Pork

1. Head
2. Clear Plate
3. Back Fat
4. Boston Butt/Shoulder
5. Loin/Tenderloin
6. Ham
7. Cheek
8. Picnic Shoulder
9. Ribs
10. Bacon/Belly
11. Hock

Pork might not be my favorite meat, but it just might be my best. I have spent hours in front of my grill, prepping ribs, and pork shoulders. As a frequent host of large parties, including a yearly rematch of Bad Santa with my hooligan high school friends, I had to start somewhere—and pork was a great place to start.

Pork has a salty flavor that cannot be mistaken. Though it can get in the way at times, pork's fat content allows it to be both juicy and tender.

Pork goes extremely well with sweet flavors, and I refer to that a lot. Pick up some local honey; it supports the beekeepers, farmers, and markets in the area. Plus, local honey tastes better. Brown sugar is delicious with pork, too. And whenever I visit a buddy in Toronto, I always pick up some Canadian maple syrup in the duty-free shop on the way home to have on hand for pork recipes.

Ribs

Ribs, in particular baby back ribs, are my best dish. If there is one thing I do, and LeBron James dunks a basketball, it is smoking baby back ribs.

I will speak in general terms when dealing with pork ribs, spare ribs, and baby backs. You want to select a cut with a good amount of fat in both cases, but it should be consistent throughout. Too much fat, especially if it is only in certain places, can make for an unappetizingly fatty bite.

We will prep our ribs the way you see them at a competition, not at the local chain barbecue restaurant. These will have just the slightest pull to them just before the meat slips and falls off the bone. If you want the meat slipping and sliding off the bone, cook them a little longer.

Tips & Techniques

Remove the membrane. That weird membrane on the back of ribs (sometimes called silver skin) can make them harder to pull off the bone and less tender. To get pit master-level results each time, remove the membrane.

Use mustard as a binder. Mustard works excellent as a binder for your rub on fatty meats such as ribs. Rub plain yellow mustard or another smooth mustard over your ribs before or after your rub. This will keep your rub on your meat and not all over your drip pan.

Use whatever liquid you like best (including beer or wine, but not liquor) for your spritz or your wrap. When watching a competition cook prep ribs with Mountain Dew, I asked why. "It's what my brother and I like and what we had, so we just started using it," he told me. I use Pepsi; my dad and brother use apple juice. Use what you like, see what other pitmasters are using and try that for a change. It's a great place to experiment.

Sauce it—just don't overdo it. Again, saucing is a real preference. At parties, I always have a plate of ribs with just a dry rub. Over the years, my ribs have gone from dry to heavily sauced, and now I only use a light sweet coating. As you will see in the recipes, we also have other ways to achieve sweetness.

Country-style ribs are ribs. Cook boneless country-style ribs the same way you would other ribs. The smoked flavor is great, and they are incredibly tender when done.

Pork shoulder

Pulled pork is something pit masters love. Not just because it's easy and useful, but because it typically means leftovers for days. Sliders, nachos, and sandwiches are all day-two and day-three renditions of the pulled-pork-leftover week. A good-size pork shoulder could feed an army—or at least an army of kids just back from baseball, gymnastics, or soccer.

When selecting your pork shoulder—also called pork butt or Boston butt—it doesn't matter if you choose one with or without a bone. Some people will tell you it does, but it's a personal preference. However, do check the fat content. You want some fat, or your pork will dry out, but too much can be overly fatty, just like ribs. The fat cap should be less than 1 inch deep.

Tips & Techniques

Inject your pork shoulder for extra moisture and flavor. Using a tea, inject your shoulder. A right shoulder will have a nice flavorful bark, but injecting will give it taste everywhere. Smoke your pork longer for a good "bark." The bark isn't just on trees or what your dog does. The bark is that delicious crust on the outside of well-smoked meat. The bark develops when the meat and rub combined with uninterrupted smoke for an extended time. A good pork shoulder will have a good, dark bark. To increase the amount of bark, smoke the pork longer, unwrapped.

Use your hands when pulling the meat— it's just easier. There are some new cool claws available that can be used for pulling pork. They keep your hands from getting hot and greasy. Fact is, though, with those, the pull never really feels right. I have a pair of cheap cotton gloves I wear under food service gloves. The gloves keep my hands from burning but let me pull the meat exactly as I like it.

Tenderloins

Pork tenderloins are among the simplest smoke preparations on the grill, but they're always impressive. I smoke a couple of tenderloins for my family every couple of weeks, and they never get tired of them. The pellet grill or smoker does a fantastic job with tenderloins, ensuring a juicy result each time.

When selecting tenderloins, as with most pork, the key is fat content. I try to limit the fat content on my tenderloins. A pellet grill will work to keep them moist and will define dried-out areas.

Tips & Techniques

If you're lazy, just smoke them. The Smoke setting of the pellet grill works great to get your meat to temperature while always keeping it moist.

Use a reverse sear. Searing is usually done first, before cooking the meat entirely. When we do it last, after fully smoking the meat, we call it a reverse sear. If your grill has an open flame option, like a flame broiler, use that; otherwise, crank up your grill's temperature as high as it will go. After smoking the tenderloins until their internal temperature reaches 135°F to 140°F, sear them off at a higher temperature until they reach 145°F, about 3 to 5 minutes per side.

Pork tenderloins are a great candidate for marinating. Teriyaki-marinated pork tenderloin tastes fantastic, and the meat can take on the marinade flavor in as little as 30 minutes.

Beef

1. Neck
2. Chuck
3. Rib
4. Short Loin
5. Sirloin
6. Tenderloin
7. Top Sirloin
8. Rump Cap
9. Round
10. Brisket
11. Shoulder Clod
12. Short Plate
13. Flank

When I think of smoking and barbecue, my mind immediately goes to beef: large brisket and tri-tip cuts, steaks over a flame. Fortunately, with today's grill technology, all of these are possible on a pellet grill.

But the dream of so many pitmasters is that perfect Texas-style brisket. We have all spent hours researching how best to achieve it: Wrapped or unwrapped? Foil or butcher paper? How long should it take? We also want steaks that even the owner of the best steakhouse would pay for—the smoke and the butter and the fire, all infused with the smell of searing meat. That's what we aim for in our backyards.

This is why I think "beef" when I think of smoking and barbecue.

Selecting beef is made easier by its grade. We'll go into this here, as well as some other tips to make you a master of low-and-slow meat cooking.

Brisket

In my experience, brisket tends to be the gold standard and the most difficult to cook on the pellet grill. Many look at the perfect brisket with reverence and hope for the day when they'll successfully achieve it. Discussions fill message boards on the bend test, the pull test, and the like. The problem with this line of thinking around brisket? Well, it's actually not that difficult to make! Brisket, just like anything else, can be perfected with practice and patience.

When selecting the perfect brisket—with both the point and flat cuts (usually separated at most butchers) intact—the key is not too much fat. If you buy a brisket with a huge fat cap, you are just going to cut it off. Also, I suggest spending the extra money on the highest grade of brisket available to you. A cheap brisket can equal a tough brisket. Brisket is not a cheap cut anyway, so spend the money for the best cut.

Tips & Techniques

Get rid of that fat cap. A large fat cap is just not delicious if you leave it on when you smoke your brisket. Use a boning knife or whatever knife you have available and cut the fat cap down to about 1/4 inch. Trimming the fat cap will decrease your brisket's fattiness, but leaving it partially there will keep the meat moist.

Wrap. Don't wrap. You choose. Both aluminum foil and butcher paper can be used for wrapping—again, it is all about preference. The one thing I will say about wrapping, however, is don't do it until after the stall, 165°F to 170°F. Wrapping too early cuts down on your bark development, and your brisket won't be as smoky.

If you don't wrap the meat, spritz it, or use a water pan. Spritzing with liquid, like apple juice or plain water, will ensure your brisket stays moist. A water pan can be used in a pellet grill just like you would in any other type of grill, but be careful not to spill it. Simply fill a metal pan with water and place it inside the grill. Have a flat drain pan; the water pan will sit there perfectly.

RUBS & MARINADES

Classic Kansas City BBQ Sauce

Preparation time: 10 Minutes

Cooking time: 15 Minutes

Servings: 24

INGREDIENTS:

- 1/4 cup yellow onion, finely chopped
- 2 tablespoons water
- 2 tablespoons vegetable oil

- 2 cups ketchup
- 1/3 cup brown sugar
- 3 cloves garlic, finely chopped
- 1 tablespoon apple cider vinegar
- 1 tablespoon tomato paste
- 1 tablespoon Worcestershire sauce
- 1 teaspoon liquid hickory smoke
- 1 teaspoon ground mustard

DIRECTIONS:

1. Put the onion in a food processor device and pulse until pureed. Add the water to the onion and pulse a few more times.
2. Use a medium saucepan, heat the oil and add the onion. When the onion is just starting to soften, add the remaining ingredients and stir well.
3. Cook the sauce at a simmer for 15 minutes, stirring occasionally.
4. Take out the pan from the heat and let it cool for thirty minutes before using or storing it in a mason jar.

NUTRITION: Calories: 799 Sodium: 595mg Dietary Fiber: 8.6g Fat: 52.7g Carbs: 74.9g Protein: 10g

Steak Sauce

Preparation time: 5 Minutes

Cooking time: 20 Minutes

Servings: 1/2 Cup

INGREDIENTS:

- 1 Tbsp. Malt vinegar
- 1/2 Tsp. Salt
- 1/2 Tsp. black pepper
- 1 Tbsp. Tomato sauce
- 2 Tbsp. brown sugar
- 1 Tsp. hot pepper sauce
- 2 Tbsp. Worcestershire sauce
- 2 Tbsp. Raspberry jam.

DIRECTIONS:

1. Pre-heat your grill for indirect cooking at 150°F
2. Place a saucepan over grates, add all your ingredients, and allow boiling.
3. Reduce Smoke's temperature and allow the sauce to simmer for 10 minutes or until the sauce is thick.

NUTRITION: Calories: 65 Carbs: 15.9g Fat: 1.3g Protein: 2.1g

Bourbon Whiskey Sauce

Preparation time: 20 Minutes

Cooking time: 25 Minutes

Servings: 3 Cups

INGREDIENTS:

- 2 cups ketchup
- 1/4 cup Worcestershire sauce
- 3/4 cup bourbon whiskey
- 1/3 cup apple cider vinegar
- 1/2 onions, minced
- 1/4 cup of tomato paste
- 2 cloves of garlic, minced
- 1/2 Tsp. Black pepper
- 1/2 cup brown sugar
- 1/2 Tbsp. Salt
- Hot pepper sauce to taste
- 1 Tbsp. Liquid smoke flavoring

DIRECTIONS:

1. Pre-heat your grill for indirect cooking at 150°F
2. Place a saucepan over grates, and then add the whiskey, garlic, and onions.
3. Simmer until the onion is translucent. Then add the other ingredients and adjust the temperature to Smoke. Simmer for 20 minutes. For a smooth sauce, sieve.

NUTRITION: Calories: 107kcal Carbs: 16.6g Fat: 1.8g Protein: 0.8g

Texas-Style Brisket Run

Preparation time: 5 Minutes

Cooking time: 0 Minutes

Servings: 1

INGREDIENTS:

- 2 Tsp. Sugar
- 2 Tbsp. Kosher salt
- 2 Tsp. Chili powder
- 2 Tbsp. Black pepper
- 2 Tbsp. Cayenne pepper
- 2 Tbsp. Powdered garlic
- 2 Tsp. Grounded cumin
- 2 Tbsp. Powdered onions
- 1/4 cup paprika, smoked

DIRECTIONS:

1. Put and combine all the ingredients in a small bowl until it is well blended.
2. Transfer to an airtight jar or container. Store in a cool place.

NUTRITION: Calories: 18kcal Carbs: 2g Fat: 1g Protein: 0.6g

Grapefruit Juice Marinade

Preparation time: 25 Minutes

Cooking time: 0 Minutes

Servings: 3 Cups

INGREDIENTS:

- 1/2 reduced-sodium soy sauce
- 3 cups grapefruit juice, unsweetened
- 1-1/2 lb. Chicken, bone and skin removed
- 1/4 brown sugar

DIRECTIONS:

1. Thoroughly mix all your ingredients in a large bowl.
2. Add the chicken and allow it to marinate for 2-3 hours before grilling.

NUTRITION: Calories: 489kcal Carbs: 21.3g Fat: 12g Protein: 24g

MEAT

Turffaloaf

Preparation time: 15 minutes

Cooking time: 1 hour

Servings: 12

INGREDIENTS:

- 1 lb ground turkey
- 1/2 pound ground buffalo
- Four pieces of day-old bread then processed into crumbs
- 1 (1 ounce) package dry onion soup mix
- 1/2 cup grated Parmesan cheese
- 2 tsp Italian seasoning
- One egg, lightly crushed
- 1/2 cup creamy dill dip
- 1/2 cup blue cheese dressing
- 2 tbsp Worcestershire sauce

DIRECTIONS:

1. Preheat oven to 375 degrees F (190 degrees C).

2. Lightly grease a 5x9 inch loaf pan.
3. In a big bowl, combine the turkey, buffalo, bread crumbs, dry onion soup mixture, Parmesan cheese, Italian seasoning, egg, dill dip, blue cheese dressing, and Worcestershire sauce.
4. Transfer into the prepared loaf pan.
5. Cover with aluminum foil, and bake for 45 minutes in the toaster.
6. Remove foil, and continue baking for 15 minutes, then to an internal temperature of 160 degrees F (70 degrees C).
7. Let stand 10 minutes before slicing.

NUTRITION: Calories: 251 Fat: 17.8g Cholesterol: 65 mg Carb: 8.3 g Protein: 14 g

Asian Glazed Cornish Hens

Preparation time: 15 minutes

Cooking time: 1 h 20 minutes

Servings: 4

INGREDIENTS:

- 3 tbsp soy sauce
- 3 tbsp teriyaki sauce
- 2 tbsp honey
- 4 tsp lemon juice
- 2 tsp garlic, minced
- 1/4 teaspoon ground black pepper
- 1/4 tsp ground ginger
- 4 Cornish hens kitchen twine

DIRECTIONS:

1. Blend soy sauce, teriyaki sauce, lemon, lemon juice, garlic, black pepper, and ginger in a large resealable plastic bag.
2. Insert Cornish hens.
3. Seal and marinate in the fridge for 2 hours.
4. Preheat oven to 400 degrees F (200 degrees C).
5. Grease a metallic rack and put it within a skillet.

6. Transfer hens out of your plastic bag to some level workout; tie legs together with kitchen twine.
7. Place hens on the ready track.
8. Pour into a small saucepan; contribute to a boil.
9. Remove from heat.
10. Roast hens at the preheated oven, occasionally basting with marinade, until juices run exact, about 1 hour.
11. Cover loosely with aluminum foil.
12. Continue roasting before an instant-read valve inserted in the uterus's thickest aspect, close to the gut, read 165 degrees F (74 degrees C), roughly 15 min longer.
13. Cover hens using aluminum foil. Let rest for 5 minutes before serving.

NUTRITION: Calories: 655 Fat: 42 g Cholesterol: 302 mg Carb: 12.8 g Protein: 53.1 g

Smoked Baby Back Ribs

Preparation time: 10 minutes

Cooking time: 2 hours

Servings: 6

Preferred Wood Pellet: Hickory

INGREDIENTS:

- 3 racks baby back ribs
- Salt and pepper to taste

DIRECTIONS:

1. Clean the ribs by removing the extra membrane that covers them. Pat dries the ribs with a clean paper towel. Whisk the baby back ribs with salt and pepper to taste. Allow resting in the fridge for at least 4 hours before cooking.
2. Once ready to cook, fire the grill to 225F.
3. Close the lid & pre-heat for 15 minutes.
4. Place the ribs on the grill grate and cook for two hours. Carefully flip the ribs halfway through the cooking time for even cooking.

NUTRITION: Calories: 1037; Protein: 92.5g; Carbs: 1.4g; Fat: 73.7g Sugar: 0.2g

Smoked Apple Pork Tenderloin

Preparation time: 10 minutes

Cooking time: 3 hours

Servings: 6

Preferred Wood Pellet: Hickory

INGREDIENTS:

- 1/2 cup apple juice
- 3 tablespoons honey
- 3 tablespoons Trailer Pork and Poultry Rub
- 1/4 cup brown sugar
- 2 tablespoons thyme leaves
- 1/2 tablespoons black pepper
- 2 pork tenderloin roasts, skin removed

DIRECTIONS:

1. In a bowl, mix apple juice, honey, pork and poultry rub, brown sugar, thyme, and black pepper. Whisk to mix everything.
2. Add the pork loins into the marinade and allow it to soak for 3 hours in the fridge.
3. Once ready to cook, fire the grill to 225F.
4. Close the lid & pre-heat for 15 minutes.

5. Place marinated pork loin on the grill grate and cook until the temperature registers to 145F. Cook for hours on low heat.

6. Meanwhile, place the marinade in a saucepan. Place the saucepan in the grill and allow it to simmer until the sauce has reduced.

7. Before taking the meat out, baste the pork with the reduced marinade.

8. Allow resting for 10 minutes before slicing.

NUTRITION: Calories: 203; Protein: 26.4g; Carbs: 15.4g; Fat: 3.6g Sugar: 14.6g

Competition Style BBQ Pork Ribs

Preparation time: 10 minutes

Cooking time: 2 hours

Servings: 6

Preferred Wood Pellet: Hard Wood Apple

INGREDIENTS:

- 2 racks of St. Louis-style ribs
- 1 cup Trailer Pork and Poultry Rub
- 1/8 cup brown sugar

- 4 tablespoons butter
- 4 tablespoons agave
- 1 bottle Trailer Sweet and Heat BBQ Sauce

DIRECTIONS:

1. Place the ribs on the working surface and remove the thin film of connective tissues covering it. In a smaller bowl, combine the Trailer Pork and Poultry Rub, brown sugar, butter, and agave. Mix until well combined.
2. Massage the rub onto the ribs and allow them to rest in the fridge for at least 2 hours.
3. When ready to cook, fire the grill to 225°F. Use desired wood pellets when cooking the ribs. Close the lid & pre-heat for 15 minutes.
4. Place the ribs on the grill grate and close the lid. Smoke for 1 hour and 30 minutes. Make sure to flip the ribs halfway through the cooking time.
5. Ten minutes before the cooking time ends, brush the ribs with BBQ sauce.
6. Take out from the grill and let it rest before slicing.

NUTRITION: Calories: 399; Protein: 47.2g; Carbs: 3.5g; Fat: 20.5g Sugar: 2.3g

Smoked Apple BBQ Ribs

Preparation time: 10 minutes

Cooking time: 2 hours

Servings: 6

Preferred Wood Pellet: Hard Wood Apple

INGREDIENTS:

- 2 racks St. Louis-style ribs
- 1/4 cup Trailer Big Game Rub

- 1 cup apple juice
- A bottle of Trailer BBQ Sauce

DIRECTIONS:

1. Place the ribs on a working surface and remove the film of connective tissues covering it.
2. In another bowl, mix the Game Rub and apple juice until well-combined.
3. Massage the rub onto the ribs and allow them to rest in the fridge for at least 2 hours.
4. When ready to cook, fire the grill to 225F. Use apple wood pellets when cooking the ribs. Close the lid & pre-heat for 15 minutes.
5. Place the ribs on the grill grate and close the lid. Smoke for 1 hour and 30 minutes. Make sure to flip the ribs halfway through the cooking time.
6. Ten minutes before the cooking time ends, brush the ribs with BBQ sauce.
7. Take out from the grill and allow it to rest before slicing.

NUTRITION: Calories: 337 Protein: 47.1g; Carbs: 4.7 g; Fat: 12.9g Sugar: 4g

Citrus-Brined Pork Roast

Preparation time: 10 minutes

Cooking time: 45 minutes

Servings: 6

Preferred Wood Pellet: Hard Wood Apple

INGREDIENTS:

- 1/2 cup of salt
- 1/4 cup brown sugar
- 3 cloves of garlic, minced
- 2 dried bay leaves
- 6 peppercorns
- 1 lemon, juiced
- 1/2 teaspoon dried fennel seeds
- 1/2 teaspoon red pepper flakes
- 1/2 cup of apple juice
- 1/2 cup of orange juice
- 5 pounds pork loin
- 2 tablespoons extra virgin olive oil

DIRECTIONS:

1. In a bowl, combine the salt, brown sugar, garlic, bay leaves, peppercorns, lemon juice, fennel seeds, pepper flakes, apple juice, and orange juice.
2. Mix to form a paste rub.
3. Rub the mixture onto the pork loin and marinate for at least 2 hours in the fridge. Add in the oil.
4. When ready to cook, fire the grill to 300F.
5. Use apple wood pellets when cooking.
6. Close the lid & pre-heat for 15 minutes.
7. Place the seasoned pork loin on the grill grate and close the lid.
8. Cook for 45 minutes.
9. Make sure to flip the pork halfway through the cooking time.

NUTRITION: Calories: 869; Protein: 97.2g; Carbs: 15.2g; Fat: 43.9g Sugar: 13g

Pork Collar and Rosemary Marinade

Preparation time: 15 minutes

Cooking time: 30 minutes

Servings: 6

Preferred Wood Pellet: Hard Wood Apple

INGREDIENTS:

- 1 pork collar, 3-4 pounds
- 3 tablespoons rosemary, fresh
- 3 shallots, minced
- 2 tablespoons garlic, chopped
- 1/2 cup bourbon
- 2 teaspoons coriander, ground
- 1 bottle of apple ale
- 1 teaspoon ground black pepper
- 2 teaspoons salt
- 3 tablespoons oil

DIRECTIONS:

1. Take a zip bag and add pepper, salt, canola oil, apple ale, bourbon, coriander, garlic, shallots, rosemary, and mix well

2. Cut meat into slabs and add them to the marinade. Let it refrigerate overnight
3. Pre-heat your smoker to 450 degrees F
4. Transfer meat to smoker and smoke for 5 minutes, lower temperature to 325 degrees F
5. Pour marinade all over and cook for 25 minutes more until the internal temperature reaches 160 degrees F
6. Serve and enjoy!

NUTRITION: Calories: 420 Fats: 26g Carbs: 4g Fiber: 2g

Roasted Ham

Preparation time: 15 minutes

Cooking time: 2 hours 15 minutes

Servings: 6

INGREDIENTS:

- 8-10 pounds ham, bone-in
- 2 tablespoons mustard, Dijon
- 1/4 cup horseradish
- 1 bottle BBQ Apricot Sauce

DIRECTIONS:

1. Pre-heat your smoker to 325 degrees F
2. Cover a roasting pan w/ foil and place the ham, transfer to the smoker, and smoke for 1 hour and 30 minutes
3. Take a small pan and add sauce, mustard and horseradish, place it over medium heat and cook for a few minutes
4. Keep it on the side
5. After 1 hour 30 minutes of smoking, glaze ham and smoke for 30 minutes more until the internal temperature reaches 135 degrees F
6. Let it rest for 20 minutes. Slice, and enjoy!

NUTRITION: Calories: 460 Fats: 43g Carbs: 10g Fiber: 1g

Fully Grilled Steak

Preparation time: 60 Minutes

Cooking time: 15 Minutes

Servings: 2

Preferred Wood Pellet: Apricot or Alder

INGREDIENTS:

- 2 USDA Choice or Prime 11/4-11/2 Inch New York Strip Steak (Approx. 12-14 ounces each) Extra Virgin Olive Oil
- 4 teaspoons of Western Love or Salt and Pepper

DIRECTIONS:

1. Remove the steak from the refrigerator; loosely cover with wrap about 45 minutes before returning to room temperature.
2. When the steak reaches room temperature, polish both sides with olive oil.
3. Season from each side of the steak with a teaspoon of rub or salt and pepper and absorb at room temperature for at least 5 minutes before grilling.
4. Configure a wood pellet smoker and grill for direct cooking using a baking grate, set the temperature high, and preheat to at least 450 ° F using the pellets.
5. Place steak on grill & cook for 2-3 minutes until browned on one side.
6. On the same side, rotate the steak 90 degrees to mark the cross grill and cook for another 2-3 minutes. Turn the steak over and bake until the desired finish is achieved.
7. 3-5 minutes for medium-rare (135 ° F internal temperature)
8. 6-7 minutes for medium (140 ° F internal temperature)
9. 8-10 minutes for medium wells (internal temperature 150 ° F)
10. Transfer the steak to a platter, loosen the tent with foil and leave for 5 minutes before serving.

NUTRITION: Calories: 240 Carbs: 0g Fat: 15g Protein: 19g

Meat Chuck Short Rib

Preparation time: 20 Minutes

Cooking time: 5-6 Hours

Servings: 2

Preferred Wood Pellet: Mesquite or Hickory Pellets

INGREDIENTS:

- English cut 4 bone slab beef chuck short rib
- 3-4 cups of mustard yellow mustard or extra virgin olive oil
- 3-5 tablespoons of Western Love

DIRECTIONS:

1. Cut the fat cap off the rib bone, leaving 1/4 inch fat, and remove the silvery skin.
2. Remove the bone's membrane and move the spoon handle below the membrane to lift the piece of meat and season the meat properly. Grab the membrane using a paper towel and pull it away from the bone.
3. Apply mustard or olive oil to all sides of the short rib slab. By rubbing it, you can season all sides.
4. Set the wood pellet smoker and grill to indirect heating and preheat to 225 ° F.

5. Insert a wood pellet smoker and grill or remote meat probe into the thickest part of the rib bone plank. If your grill does not have a meat probe or you do not have a remote meat probe, use an instant reading digital thermometer to read the internal temperature while cooking.
6. Place the short rib bone on the grill with the bone side down and smoke at 225 ° F for 5 hours.
7. If the ribs have not reached an internal temperature of at least 195 ° F after 5 hours, increase the pit temperature to 250 ° F until the internal temperature reaches 195 ° to 205 ° F.
8. Place the smoked short rib bone under the loose foil tent for 15 minutes before serving.

NUTRITION: Calories: 357 Carbs: 0gFat: 22gProtein: 37g

Texas Style Brisket Flat

Preparation time: 45 Minutes (Additional Marinade, Optional)

Cooking time: 5-6 Hours

Servings: 8

Preferred Wood Pellet: Oak or mesquite

INGREDIENTS:

- 6 1/2 lbs. beef brisket flat
- 1/2 cup of roasted garlic flavored extra virgin olive oil
- 1/2 Cup Texas Style Brisket Love or Favorite Brisket Love

DIRECTIONS:

1. Cut off the fat cap of the brisket and remove the silver skin.
2. Rub all sides of the trimmed meat with olive oil.
3. Put the rub to all sides of the brisket so that it is entirely covered by the rub.
4. Wrap the brisket twice with plastic wrap and cool overnight to allow the meat to penetrate. Or, if needed, you can cook the brisket immediately.
5. Remove the brisket from the refrigerator and insert a wood pellet smoker and grill. If your grill does not have

a meat probe, features, or does not have a remote meat probe, use an instant reading digital thermometer to read the internal temperature while cooking.

6. Set wood pellet smoker and grill for indirect cooking and preheat to 250 ° F.

7. Smoke the brisket at 250 ° F until the internal temperature reaches 160 ° F (about 4 hours).

8. Take out the brisket from the grill, wrap it twice in sturdy aluminum foil, keep the meat probe in place and return to the smoking grill.

9. Raise the pit temperature to 325 ° F and cook the brisket for another 2 hours until the internal temperature reaches 205 ° F.

10. Remove the brisket with foil, wrap it with a towel and put it in the cooler. Let sit in the cooler for 2-4 hours before slicing into cereals and serving.

NUTRITION: Calories: 180 Carbs: 2g Fat: 9g Protein: 23g

Smoked Pulled Lamb Sliders

Preparation time: 10 minutes

Cooking time: 3 hours

Servings: 7

Preferred Wood Pellet: Hard Wood Mesquite

INGREDIENTS:

- 5 lb. lamb shoulder, boneless
- 1/2 cup olive oil
- 1/4 cup dry rub
- 10-ounce spritz
- The Dry Rub
- 1/3 cup kosher salt
- 1/3 cup pepper, ground
- 1-1/3 cup garlic, granulated
- The Spritz
- 4 ounce Worcestershire sauce
- 6-ounce apple cider vinegar

DIRECTIONS:

1. Preheat the wood pellet smoker with a water bath to 250°F.

2. Trim any fat from the lamb, then rub with oil and dry rub.
3. Place the lamb on the smoker for 90 minutes, then spritz with a spray bottle.
4. Transfer the lamb shoulder to a foil pan with the remaining spritz liquid and cover tightly with foil.
5. Place back in the smoker and smoke until the internal temperature reaches 200°F.
6. Let it rest serving with slaw, bun, or aioli.
7. Enjoy!

NUTRITION: Calories: 339, Fat: 22g, Carbs: 16g,Protein: 18g

Lamb Meatballs

Preparation time: 10 minutes

Cooking time: 1 hr.

Servings: 5

Preferred Wood Pellet: Hard Wood Mesquite

INGREDIENTS:

- Lb. lamb shoulder, ground
- Garlic cloves, finely diced
- Tbsp. shallot, diced
- 1 Tbsp. salt
- 1 egg
- 1/2 Tbsp. pepper
- 1/2 Tbsp. cumin
- 1/2 Tbsp. smoked paprika
- 1/4 Tbsp. red pepper flakes
- 1/4 Tbsp. cinnamon, ground
- 1/4 cup panko breadcrumbs

DIRECTIONS:

1. Set the wood pellet smoker to 250°F using a fruitwood.
2. In a mixing bowl, combine all meatball ingredients until well mixed.

3. Form small-sized balls and place them on a baking sheet. Place the baking sheet in the smoker and smoke until the internal temperature reaches 160°F.
4. Remove from the smoker and serve.
5. Enjoy.

NUTRITION: Calories: 73, Fat: 5g, Carbs: 2g, Protein: 5g

Crown Rack of Lamb

Preparation time: 10 minutes

Cooking time: 30 minutes

Servings: 6

Preferred Wood Pellet: Hard Wood Mesquite

INGREDIENTS:

- 2 racks of lamb, drenched
- Tbsp. garlic, crushed
- 1 Tbsp. rosemary, finely chopped
- 1/4 cup olive oil
- Feet twine

DIRECTIONS:

1. Rinse the racks with cold water, then pat them dry with a paper towel.
2. Lay the racks on a flat board, then score between each bone, about 1/4 inch down.
3. In a mixing bowl, mix garlic, rosemary, and oil, then generously brush on the lamb.
4. Take each lamb rack and bend it into a semicircle forming a crown-like shape.

5. Use the twine to wrap the racks about 4 times, starting from the base to the top. Make sure you tie the twine tightly to keep the racks together.
6. Preheat the wood pellet to 400-450°F, then place the lamb racks on a baking dish.
7. Cook for 10 minutes, then reduces the temperature to 300°F. Cook for 20 more minutes or until the internal temperature reaches 130°F.
8. Remove the lamb rack from the wood pellet and let rest for 15 minutes.
9. Serve when hot with veggies and potatoes.

NUTRITION: Calories: 390, Fat: 35g, Protein: 17g

Smoking Leg of Lamb

Preparation time: 15 minutes

Cooking time: 4 hours

Servings: 6

Preferred Wood Pellet: Hard Wood Mesquite

INGREDIENTS:

- Leg lamb, boneless
- 4 garlic cloves, minced
- Tbsp. salt
- 1 Tbsp. black pepper, freshly ground
- Tbsp. oregano
- 1 Tbsp. thyme
- 2 Tbsp. olive oil

DIRECTIONS:

1. Trim any excess fat from lamb and tie the lamb using twine to form a nice roast.
2. In a mixing bowl, mix garlic, spices, and oil. Rub all over the lamb, wrap with a plastic bag then refrigerate for an hour to marinate.

3. Place the lamb on a smoker set at 250°F. Smoke the lamb for 4 hours or until the internal temperature reaches 145°F.
4. Remove from the smoker and let rest to cool. Serve and enjoy.

NUTRITION: Calories: 350, Fat: 16g, Carbs: 3g, Protein: 49g

Teriyaki Beef Jerky

Preparation time: 10 mins

Cooking time: 1 hr.

Servings: 5

Preferred Wood Pellet: Apricot or Alder

INGREDIENTS:

- 3 lbs beef high beef
- 1 1/2 cup teriyaki sauce
- 1/2 cup soy sauce
- 1 teaspoon garlic powder

- 1 teaspoon onion powder
- 3 tsp sesame seeds
- 2 teaspoon salt
- 3 tablespoons of rice wine vinegar
- 2 tablespoon brown sugar

DIRECTIONS:

1. Cut all of the fat off the steak and slice into thin strips, about 1/8" inches. This is simpler when meat is stiffened from the freezer.
2. Dissolve the brown sugar in the vinegar on very low heat. Don't omit the vinegar as it is necessary to maintain the meat.
3. Coat the beef at the sugar/vinegar mixture and simmer for one hour
4. Mix together the Teriyaki sauce, Soy sauce, garlic powder, and onion powder
5. Coat the steak in the sauce mixture and refrigerate overnight
6. Preheat your smoker to 190°F-230°F, lid closed for 15 minutes.
7. Remove the steak out of the sauce mixture. Tap excess moisture with a paper towel and lay on the smoker grate.
8. Cook meat for two 1/2 hours
9. Examine the feel of the thinnest bits, and remove from oven when prepared
10. During the next hour, then the thicker bits will slowly reach the ideal texture.

11. Eliminate leftover meat from the oven
12. With grout and pestle, grind together sesame seeds and salt 16. Sprinkle the salt and sesame mixture over the jerky
13. Allow beef to dry in a cool area for a further 12 hours prior to storing in a landfill. Should continue for 2-3 weeks.

NUTRITION: Calories 204, protein 18.7g, carbs 2g, fat 13g, cholesterol 55.3g, sodium 791mg.

BBQ Beef Jerky

Preparation time: 30 mins

Cooking time: 6 hrs

Servings: 8

Preferred Wood Pellet: Apricot or Alder

INGREDIENTS:

- 1 1/2 pounds flank steak
- 1/2 cup ketchup
- 1/3 cup red wine vinegar
- 1 tablespoon dry mustard
- 1/4 cup brown sugar
- 1 tablespoon onion powder
- 2 tablespoon hickory liquid smoke
- 2 tablespoon Morton's curing salt
- 1/2 tsp garlic powder
- 1/4 tsp cayenne pepper

DIRECTIONS:

1. Reduce the fat off the beef and put trimmed beef in the freezer until it's firm but not frozen (1-2 hours).

2. Slice beef across the grain of the meat, to strands as long and lean as you can, under 1/8". Over low heat, dissolve the brown sugar into the red wine vinegar

3. Add all the other elements (except the beef) and stir until smooth and combined

4. Remove sauce mixture from the cooker, add other seasonings to taste

5. Coat meat in sauce mixture, refrigerate overnight

6. Take your oven stands and line them with foil

7. Organize the beef strips on the smoker grate, so there are no overlaps

8. Preheat your smoker to 190°F-230°F, lid closed for 15 minutes.

9. Cook meat for 3-4 hours until endings of meat start to unwind and feel it is proper. This will occur sooner if your toaster reaches 230° F or greater.

10. Remove meat from the oven and then tap excess moisture or fat with a paper towel.

11. Hang in a cool, dry area immediately.

12. Store in a plastic container should keep for up to 3 weeks

NUTRITION: Calories 317 protein 20g carbs 49g fat 4.7g cholesterol 25.3mg sodium 5422mg.

Classic Turkey Jerky

Preparation time: 15 mins

Cooking time: 4 hrs.

Servings: 8

Preferred Wood Pellet: Apricot or Alder

INGREDIENTS:

- 1 lb. skinless, boneless turkey breastfeeding
- 2 tablespoon mesquite liquid smoke
- 2 tablespoon soy sauce
- 1/4 tsp Tabasco sauce
- 1/4 cup Worcestershire sauce
- 2 tsp brown sugar
- 1 tablespoon onion powder
- 2 teaspoon garlic powder
- 1 tablespoon kosher salt
- 1/2 tsp nutmeg
- 1 package wooden skewers

DIRECTIONS:

1. Trim any fat off the turkey meat
2. Slice turkey to 1/8" thick strips (this is simpler if stiffened from the freezer)

3. Blend ingredients in a mixing bowl to Create a marinade
4. Coat the turkey with the marinade and refrigerate overnight
5. Remove turkey strips from marinade and tap excess liquid with a paper towel
6. Thread turkey strips on bamboo skewers by pushing the skewer through a single end of the strip and the other so that it creates a 'sail' contour
7. Hang the skewers on the smoker grate so that air flows around the meat
8. Preheat your smoker to 190°F-230°F, lid closed for 15 minutes.
9. Cook jerky for 3 hours until chewy but tender
10. Remove from oven and Permit jerky to air-dry overnight in a cool, dry area
11. Store jerky in a sterile container or purse. Should keep 2-3 weeks

NUTRITION: Calories 208 protein 15g carbs 22.1g fat 6.5g cholesterol 48mg sodium 2186mg

Sweet and Hot Turkey Jerky

Preparation time: 30 mins

Cooking time: 8 hrs.

Servings: 8

Preferred Wood Pellet: Apricot or Alder

INGREDIENTS:

- 2 pounds skinless turkey breast
- 1/2 cup soy sauce
- 1/4 cup sesame oil
- 1/4 cup brown sugar
- 2 tablespoon honey
- 1 tablespoon chipotle chili powder
- 2 tbsp sesame seeds
- 2 teaspoon ground pepper
- 2 tbsp minced ginger
- 1 tablespoon minced garlic

DIRECTIONS:

1. Trim any fat off the meat
2. Stiffen beef in the freezer for about an hour, then slit into 1/8" thick strips

3. In a saucepan, use 1 tablespoon of sesame oil to brown the garlic and ginger
4. Mix the ginger and garlic with the remaining ingredients
5. Coat both sides of turkey strips together with the marinade
6. Marinate turkey for 4-6 hours in the fridge
7. Preheat your smoker to 190°F-230°F, lid closed for 15 minutes.
8. Lay turkey strips on the smoker grate, preventing overlaps
9. Cook jerky for 3-4 hours until elastic but 'snaps' when flexed
10. Remove from oven and Permit jerky to air-dry overnight in a cool, dry area
11. Store in a sterile container at room temperature. Should keep about two months.

NUTRITION: Calories 111 protein 13.6g carbs 2.9g fat 4.8g cholesterol 48mq sodium 786mg.

Drunken Chicken Jerky

Preparation time: 20 mins

Cooking time: 3 hrs.

Servings: 6

Preferred Wood Pellet: Apricot or Alder

INGREDIENTS:

- 1 lb. lean chicken breast
- 1/4 cup teriyaki sauce
- 1/4 cup tightly packed brown sugar
- 1/4 cup soy sauce
- 1/2 cup red wine
- 1/4 cup tequila
- 1/4 cup beer
- 1 tablespoon liquid smoke
- 1 teaspoon Tabasco sauce

DIRECTIONS:

1. Cutaway any excess fat from the chicken
2. Freeze turkey for 1-2 hours stiffen
3. Slice turkey into long, thin strips, about 1/8" broad
4. Blend ingredients in a mixing bowl to create a marinade. Add pepper and salt to taste.

5. Coat chicken in marinade and allow to sit at room temperature overnight
6. Remove turkey strips from marinade
7. Preheat your smoker to 190°F, lid closed for 15 minutes.
8. Lay chicken strips on the smoker grate, preventing overlaps
9. Cook jerky for 3 hours until the feel is elastic; however, 'cracks' when flexed
10. Remove from oven and Permit jerky to air-dry overnight in a cool, dry area
11. Store jerky in a sterile sealed container. Alcohol is a powerful preservative; also, this jerky should endure for as long as six weeks.

NUTRITION: Calories 86 protein 14.3g carbs 2.5g fat 1.7g cholesterol 52mg sodium 1189mg.

VEGETABLES

Roasted Green Beans with Bacon

Preparation time: 15 minutes

Cooking time: 20 minutes

Servings: 4/6

Preferred Wood Pellet: Hickory or Apple

INGREDIENTS:

- 1-pound green beans
- 4 strips bacon, cut into small pieces
- 4 tablespoons extra virgin olive oil
- 2 cloves garlic, minced
- 1 teaspoon salt

DIRECTIONS:

1. Fire the grill to 400F. Use desired wood pellets when cooking. Keep lid unopened and let it preheat for at most 15 minutes
2. Toss all ingredients on a sheet tray and spread out evenly.
3. Place the tray on the grill grate and roast for 20 minutes.

NUTRITION: Calories: 65 Cal Fat: 5.3 g Carbohydrates: 3 gProtein: 1.3 g Fiber: 0 g

Smoked Watermelon

Preparation time: 15 minutes

Cooking time: 50 minutes

Servings: 4/6

Preferred Wood Pellet: Hickory or Apple

INGREDIENTS:

- 1 small seedless watermelon
- Balsamic vinegar
- Wooden skewers

DIRECTIONS:

1. Slice ends of small seedless watermelons
2. Slice the watermelon into 1-inch cubes. Put the cubes in a container and drizzle vinegar on the cubes of watermelon.
3. Preheat, the smoker to 225°F.
4. Place the cubes on the skewers.
5. Place the skewers on the smoker rack for 50 minutes.
6. Cook
7. Remove the skewers.
8. Serve!

NUTRITION: Calories: 20 Cal Fat: 0 g Carbohydrates: 4 g Protein: 1 g Fiber: 0.2 g

Grilled Corn with Honey Butter

Preparation time: 15 minutes

Cooking time: 10 minutes

Servings: 4/6

INGREDIENTS:

- 6 pieces corn, husked
- 2 tablespoons olive oil
- Salt and pepper to taste
- 1/2 cup butter, room temperature
- 1/2 cup honey

DIRECTIONS:

1. Fire the grill to 350F. Use desired wood pellets when cooking. Keep lid unopened to preheat until 15 minutes
2. Coat corn with oil and add salt and pepper
3. Place the corn on the grill grate and cook for 10 minutes. Make sure to flip the corn halfway through the cooking time for even cooking.
4. Meanwhile, mix the butter and honey in a small bowl. Set aside.
5. Remove corn from grill and coat with honey butter sauce

NUTRITION: Calories: 387 Cal Fat: 21.6 g Carbohydrates: 51.2 g Protein: 5 g Fiber: 0 g

Smoked Mushrooms

Preparation time: 20 minutes

Cooking time: 2 hours

Servings: 4/6

Preferred Wood Pellet: Hickory or Apple

INGREDIENTS:

- 6-12 large Portobello mushrooms
- Sea salt
- Black pepper
- Extra virgin olive oil

- Herbs de Provence

DIRECTIONS:

1. Preheat the smoker to 200°F while adding water and wood chips to the smoker bowl and tray, respectively.
2. Wash and dry mushrooms
3. Massage the mushrooms with olive oil, salt and pepper seasoning with herbs in a bowl.
4. Place the mushrooms with the cap side down on the smoker rack. Smoke the mushrooms for 2 hours while adding water and wood chips to the smoker after every 60 minutes.
5. Remove the mushrooms and serve

NUTRITION: Calories: 106 Cal Fat: 6 g Carbohydrates: 5 g Protein: 8 g Fiber: 0.9 g

Smoked Cherry Tomatoes

Preparation time: 20 minutes

Cooking time: 90 minutes

Servings: 4/6

Preferred Wood Pellet: Hickory or Apple

INGREDIENTS:

- 2 pints of tomatoes

DIRECTIONS:

1. Preheat the electric smoker to 225°F while adding wood chips and water to the smoker.
2. Clean the tomatoes with clean water and dry them off properly.
3. Place the tomatoes on the pan and place the pan in the smoker.
4. Smoke for 90 minutes while adding water and wood chips to the smoker.

NUTRITION: Calories: 16 Cal Fat: 0 g Carbohydrates: 3 g Protein: 1 g Fiber: 1 g

Smoked and Smashed New Potatoes

Preparation time: 5 minutes

Cooking time: 60 minutes

Servings: 4/6

Preferred Wood Pellet: Hickory or Apple

INGREDIENTS:

- 1-1/2 pounds small new red potatoes or fingerlings
- Extra virgin olive oil
- Sea salt and black pepper
- 2 Tbsp. softened butter

DIRECTIONS:

1. Let the potatoes dry. Once dried, put in a pan and coat with salt, pepper, and extra virgin olive oil.
2. Place the potatoes on the top rack of the smoker.
3. Smoke for 60 minutes.
4. Once done, take them out and smash each one
5. Mix with butter and season

NUTRITION: Calories: 258 Cal Fat: 2.0 g Carbohydrates: 15.5 g Protein: 4.1 g Fiber: 1.5 g

POULTRY

Buffalo Chicken Wings

Preparation time: 15 Minutes

Cooking time: 25 Minutes

Preferred Wood Pellet: Oak or Alder

Servings: 6

INGREDIENTS:

- 2 lb. chicken wings
- 1/2 cup sweet, spicy dry rub
- 2/3 cup buffalo sauce
- Celery, chopped

DIRECTIONS:

1. Start your wood pellet grill.
2. Set it to 450 degrees F.
3. Sprinkle the chicken wings w/ the dry rub.
4. Place on the grill rack.
5. Cook for 10 minutes per side.
6. Brush with the buffalo sauce.
7. Grill for another 5 minutes.
8. Dip each wing in the buffalo sauce.
9. Sprinkle the celery on top.

NUTRITION: Calories 935 Total fat 53g Saturated fat 15g Protein 107gSodium 320mg

Sweet and Sour Chicken

Preparation time: 30 Minutes

Cooking time: 3 Hours

Servings: 4

Preferred Wood Pellet: Oak or Alder

INGREDIENTS:

- Eight chicken drumsticks
- 1/4 cup soy sauce
- 1 cup ketchup
- Two tablespoons rice wine vinegar
- Two tablespoons lemon juice
- Two tablespoons honey
- Two tablespoons garlic, minced
- Two tablespoons ginger, minced
- One tablespoon sweet-spicy dry rub
- Three tablespoons brown sugar

DIRECTIONS:

1. Combine all the sauce fixings in a bowl.
2. Mix well.
3. Take half of the mixture, transfer to another bowl and refrigerate.

4. Add the chicken to the bowl with the remaining sauce.
5. Toss to coat evenly.
6. Cover and refrigerate for 4 hours.
7. When it's cook, take out the chicken from the fridge. Discard the marinade.
8. Turn on your wood pellet grill.
9. Set it to smoke.
10. Set the temperature to 225 degrees F.
11. Smoke the chicken for 3 hours.
12. Serve the chicken with the reserved sauce.

NUTRITION: Calories 935 Total fat 53g Saturated fat 15g Protein 107gSodium 320mg

Smoked Chicken with Perfect Poultry Rub

Preparation time: 20 minutes

Cooking time: 3 hours 15 minutes.

Servings: 2

Preferred Wood Pellet: Apricot or Alder

INGREDIENTS:

- 2 Tbsp. of onion, powder
- 1/4 cup of black pepper, freshly ground
- 2 Tbsp. of dry mustard
- 3/4 cup of paprika
- 4pound chicken
- 3 lemons
- 2 Tsp. of cayenne
- 1/4 cup of sugar
- 1/4 cup of celery salt

DIRECTIONS:

1. In a bowl, mix the onion powder, paprika, black pepper, dry mustard, cayenne, sugar, celery, salt, and 2 lemons.
2. Add your chicken to the rub and slice some parts so that the ingredients will find their way in.
3. Preheat the grill for 15 minutes at 225°F.
4. Place the coated chicken on the preheated grill and smoke for 3 hours or until the internal temperature reads 160°F.
5. Allow chicken to cool, and then serve.

NUTRITION: Calories: 255kcal,Protein: 35g,Carbs: 42g, Fat: 35g.

Honey Glazed Whole Chicken

Preparation time: 30 Minutes

Cooking time: 4 Hours

Servings: 4

Preferred Wood Pellet: Oak or Alder

INGREDIENTS:

- One tablespoon honey
- Four tablespoons butter
- Three tablespoons lemon juice
- One whole chicken, giblets trimmed
- Four tablespoons chicken seasoning

DIRECTIONS:

1. Set your wood pellet grill to smoke.
2. Set it to 225 degrees F.
3. In a pan over low heat, increase the honey and butter. Pour in the lemon juice.
4. Add the seasoning.
5. Cook for 1 minute, stirring.
6. Add the chicken to the grill.
7. Smoke for 8 minutes.
8. Flip the chicken and brush with the honey mixture.

9. Smoke for 3 hours, brushing the sauce every 40 minutes.

10. Let rest for 5 minutes before serving.

NUTRITION: Calories 935 Total fat 53g Saturated fat 15g Protein 107g Sodium 320mg

Chicken Lollipops

Preparation time: 30 Minutes

Cooking time: 2 Hours 15 minutes

Servings: 6

Preferred Wood Pellet: Oak or Alder

INGREDIENTS:

- 12 chicken lollipops
- Chicken seasoning
- Ten tablespoons butter, sliced into 12 cubes
- 1 cup barbecue sauce
- 1 cup hot sauce

DIRECTIONS:

1. Turn on your wood pellet grill.
2. Set it to 300 degrees F.
3. Then season the chicken with the chicken seasoning.
4. Arrange the chicken in a baking pan.
5. Put the butter cubes on top of each chicken.
6. Cook the chicken lollipops for 2 hours, basting with the melted butter in the baking pan every 20 minutes.
7. Pour in the barbecue sauce and hot sauce over the chicken.
8. Grill for 15 minutes.

NUTRITION: Calories 935 Total fat 53g Saturated fat 15g Protein 107gSodium 320mg

Asian Wings

Preparation time: 30 Minutes

Cooking time: 1 Hour 20 minutes

Servings: 6

Preferred Wood Pellet: Oak or Alder

INGREDIENTS:

- One teaspoon honey
- One teaspoon soy sauce
- Two teaspoon rice vinegar
- 1/2 cup hoisin sauce
- Two teaspoon sesame oil
- One teaspoon ginger, minced
- One teaspoon garlic, minced
- One teaspoon green onion, chopped
- 1 cup hot water
- 2 lb. chicken wings

DIRECTIONS:

1. Combine all the sauce fixings in a large bowl. Mix well.
2. Transfer 1/3 of the sauce to another bowl and refrigerate.
3. Add the chicken wings to the remaining sauce.

4. Cover and refrigerate for 2 hours.
5. Turn on your wood pellet grill.
6. Set it to 300 degrees F.
7. Add the wings to a grilling basket. Cook for 1 hour.
8. Heat the reserved sauce in a pan.
9. Bring to your boil and then simmer for 10 minutes.
10. Brush the chicken with the remaining sauce.
11. Grill for another 10 minutes.
12. Let rest for 5 minutes before serving.

NUTRITION: Calories 935 Total fat 53g Saturated fat 15g Protein 107g Sodium 320mg

Lemon Chicken in Foil Packet

Preparation time: 5 Minutes

Cooking time: 25 Minutes

Servings: 4

Preferred Wood Pellet: Oak or Alder

INGREDIENTS:

- Four chicken fillets
- Three tablespoons melted butter
- One garlic, minced
- 1-1/2 teaspoon dried Italian seasoning
- Salt and pepper to taste
- One lemon, sliced

DIRECTIONS:

1. Turn on your wood pellet grill.
2. Keep the lid open while burning for 5 minutes.
3. Preheat it to 450 degrees F.
4. Add the chicken fillet on top of foil sheets.
5. In a bowl, mix the butter, garlic, seasoning, salt, and pepper.
6. Brush the chicken with this mixture.
7. Put the lemon slices on top.

8. Wrap the chicken with the foil.
9. Grill each side for 7 to 10 minutes per side.

NUTRITION: Calories 935 Total fat 53g Saturated fat 15g Protein 107gSodium 320mg

Herb Roasted Turkey

Preparation time: 15 Minutes

Cooking time: 3 Hours 30 Minutes

Servings: 12

Preferred Wood Pellet: Hickory

INGREDIENTS:

- 14 pounds turkey, cleaned
- 2 tablespoons chopped mixed herbs

- Pork and poultry rub as needed
- 1/4 teaspoon ground black pepper
- 3 tablespoons butter, unsalted, melted
- 8 tablespoons butter, unsalted, softened
- 2 cups chicken broth

DIRECTIONS:

1. Clean the turkey by removing the giblets, wash it inside out, pat dry with paper towels, then place it on a roasting pan and tuck the turkey wings by tiring with butcher's string.

2. Switch on the grill, fill the grill hopper with Hickory flavored wood pellets, power the grill on by using the control panel, select 'smoke' on the temperature dial, or set the temperature to 325 degrees F and let it preheat for a minimum of 15 minutes.

3. Meanwhile, prepare herb butter, take a small bowl, place the softened butter in it, add black pepper and mixed herbs and beat until fluffy.

4. Place some of the prepared herb butter underneath the turkey's skin by using a wooden spoon handle and massage the skin to distribute butter evenly.

5. Then rub the turkey's exterior with melted butter, season with pork and poultry rub, and pour the broth in the roasting pan.

6. When the grill has preheated, open the lid, place the roasting pan containing turkey on the grill grate, shut the grill and smoke for 3 hours and 30 minutes until the

internal temperature reaches 165 degrees F and the top has turned golden brown.

7. When done, transfer turkey to a cutting board, rest for 30 minutes, then carve it into slices and serve.

NUTRITION: Calories: 154.6; Fat: 3.1 g;Carbs: 8.4 g; Protein: 28.8 g

Turkey Legs

Preparation time: 10 Minutes

Cooking time: 5 Hours

Servings: 4

Preferred Wood Pellet: Hickory

INGREDIENTS:

- 4 turkey legs
- For the Brine:
- 1/2 cup curing salt
- 1 tablespoon whole black peppercorns
- 1 cup BBQ rub
- 1/2 cup brown sugar
- 2 bay leaves
- 2 teaspoons liquid smoke
- 16 cups of warm water
- 4 cups ice
- 8 cups of cold water

DIRECTIONS:

1. Prepare the brine and for this, take a large stockpot, place it over high heat, pour warm water in it, add

peppercorn, bay leaves, and liquid smoke, stir in salt, sugar, and BBQ rub and bring it to a boil.

2. Remove pot from heat, bring it to room temperature, then pour in cold water, add ice cubes and let the brine chill in the refrigerator.

3. Then add turkey legs in it, submerge them completely, and let soak for 24 hours in the refrigerator.

4. After 24 hours, remove turkey legs from the brine, rinse well and pat dry with paper towels.

5. When ready to cook, switch on the grill, fill the grill hopper with hickory flavored wood pellets, power the grill on by using the control panel, select 'smoke' on the temperature dial, or set the temperature to 250 degrees F and let it preheat for a minimum of 15 minutes.

6. When the grill has preheated, open the lid, place turkey legs on the grill grate, shut the grill, and smoke for 5 hours until nicely browned and the internal temperature reaches 165 degrees F. Serve immediately.

NUTRITION: Calories: 416;Fat: 13.3 g; Carbs: 0 g; Protein: 69.8 g

Turkey Breast

Preparation time: 12 Hours

Cooking time: 8 Hours

Servings: 6

Preferred Wood Pellet: Hard Wood Mesquite

INGREDIENTS:

- For The Brine:
- 2 pounds turkey breast, deboned
- 2 tablespoons ground black pepper
- 1/4 cup salt
- 1 cup brown sugar
- 4 cups cold water
- For The BBQ Rub:
- 2 tablespoons dried onions
- 2 tablespoons garlic powder
- 1/4 cup paprika
- 2 tablespoons ground black pepper
- 1 tablespoon salt
- 2 tablespoons brown sugar
- 2 tablespoons red chili powder
- 1 tablespoon cayenne pepper
- 2 tablespoons sugar
- 2 tablespoons ground cumin

DIRECTIONS:

1. Prepare the brine and for this, take a large bowl, add salt, black pepper, and sugar in it, pour in water, and stir until sugar has dissolved.
2. Place turkey breast in it, submerge it entirely and let it soak for a minimum of 12 hours in the refrigerator.

3. Meanwhile, prepare the BBQ rub and for this, take a small bowl, place all of its ingredients in it and then stir until combined, set aside until required.
4. Then remove turkey breast from the brine and season well with the prepared BBQ rub.
5. When ready to cook, switch on the grill, fill the grill hopper with apple-flavored wood pellets, power the grill on by using the control panel, select 'smoke' on the temperature dial and let it preheat for a minimum of 15 minutes.
6. When the grill has preheated, open the lid, place turkey breast on the grill grate, shut the grill, change the smoking temperature to 225 degrees F, and smoke for 8 hours until the internal temperature reaches 160 degrees F.
7. When done, transfer turkey to a cutting board, let it rest for 10 minutes, then cut it into slices and serve.

NUTRITION: Calories: 250; Fat: 5 g;Carbs: 31 g; Protein: 18 g

SEAFOOD

Juicy Smoked Salmon

Preparation time: 20 minutes

Cooking time: 50 minutes

Servings: 5

Preferred Wood Pellet: Oak or Alder

INGREDIENTS:

- 1/2 cup of sugar
- 2 tablespoon salt
- 2 tablespoons crushed red pepper flakes
- 1/2 cup fresh mint leaves, chopped
- 1/4 cup brandy
- 1 (4 pounds) salmon, bones removed
- 2 cups alder wood pellets, soaked in water

DIRECTIONS:

1. Take a medium-sized bowl and add brown sugar, crushed red pepper flakes, mint leaves, salt, and brandy until a paste forms
2. Rub the paste all over your salmon and wrap the salmon with a plastic wrap
3. Allow them to chill overnight
4. Preheat your smoker to 220 degrees Fahrenheit and add wood Pellets
5. Transfer the salmon to the smoker rack and cook smoke for 45 minutes
6. Once the salmon has turned red-brown and the flesh flakes off easily, take it out and serve!

NUTRITION: Calories: 370 Fats: 28g Carbs: 1g Fiber: 0g

Peppercorn Tuna Steaks

Preparation time: 20 minutes

Cooking time: 1 hour

Servings: 3

Preferred Wood Pellet: Oak or Alder

INGREDIENTS:

- 1/4 cup of salt
- 2 pounds yellowfin tuna
- 1/4 cup Dijon mustard
- Freshly ground black pepper
- 2 tablespoons peppercorn

DIRECTIONS:

1. Take a large-sized container and dissolve salt in warm water (enough water to cover fish)
2. Transfer tuna to the brine and cover, refrigerate for 8 hours
3. Preheat your smoker to 250 degrees Fahrenheit with your preferred wood
4. Remove tuna from bring and pat it dry
5. Transfer to grill pan and spread Dijon mustard all over
6. Season with pepper and sprinkle peppercorn on top
7. Transfer tuna to smoker and smoker for 1 hour

8. Enjoy!

NUTRITION: Calories: 707 Fats: 57g Carbs: 10g Fiber: 2g

Stuffed Shrimp Tilapia

Preparation time: 20 minutes

Cooking time: 45 minutes

Servings: 5

Preferred Wood Pellet: Oak or Alder

INGREDIENTS:

- 5 ounces fresh, farmed tilapia fillets
- 2 tablespoons extra virgin olive oil
- 1 and 1/2 teaspoons smoked paprika

- Shrimp stuffing
- 1-pound shrimp, cooked and deveined
- 1 tablespoon salted butter
- 1 cup red onion, diced
- 1 cup Italian breadcrumbs
- 1/2 cup mayonnaise
- 1 large egg, beaten
- 2 teaspoons fresh parsley, chopped
- 1 and 1/2 teaspoons salt and pepper

DIRECTIONS:

1. Take a food processor and add shrimp, chop them up
2. Take a skillet and place it over medium-high heat, add butter and allow it to melt
3. Sauté the onions for 3 minutes
4. Add chopped shrimp with cooled Sautéed onion alongside remaining ingredients listed under stuffing ingredients and transfer to a bowl
5. Cover the mixture & allow it to refrigerate for 60 minutes
6. Rub both sides of the fillet with olive oil
7. Spoon 1/3 cup of the stuffing to the fillet
8. Flatten out the stuffing onto the bottom half of the fillet and fold the Tilapia in half
9. Secure with 2 toothpicks
10. Dust each fillet with smoked paprika and Old Bay seasoning
11. Preheat your smoker to 400 degrees Fahrenheit

12. Add your preferred wood Pellets and transfer the fillets to a non-stick grill tray
13. Transfer to your smoker and smoker for 30-45 minutes until the internal temperature reaches 145 degrees Fahrenheit
14. Allow fish to rest for 5 minutes and enjoy!

NUTRITION: Calories: 620 Fats: 50g Carbs: 6g Fiber: 1g

Togarashi Smoked Salmon

Preparation time: 20 minutes

Cooking time: 4 hours

Servings: 10

Preferred Wood Pellet: Oak or Alder

INGREDIENTS:

- Salmon filet - 2 large

- Togarashi for seasoning
- For Brine:
- Brown sugar - 1 cup
- Water - 4 cups
- Kosher salt – 1/3 cup

DIRECTIONS:

1. Remove all the thorns from the fish filet.
2. Mix all the brine ingredients until the brown sugar is dissolved completely.
3. Put the mix in a big bowl and add the filet to it.
4. Leave the bowl to refrigerate for 16 hours.

5. After 16 hours, remove the salmon from this mix. Wash and dry it.
6. Place the salmon in the refrigerator for another 2-4 hours. (This step is essential. DO NOT SKIP IT.)
7. Season your salmon filet with Togarashi.
8. Start the wood pellet grill with the 'smoke' option and place the salmon on it.
9. Smoke for 4 hours.
10. Remove from the grill and serve it warm with a side dish of your choice.

NUTRITION: Carbohydrates: 19g Protein: 10 g Fat: 6 g Sodium: 3772 mg Cholesterol: 29 mg

BBQ Oysters

Preparation time: 1-2 hours

Cooking time: 16 minutes

Servings: 4-6

Preferred Wood Pellet: Oak or Alder

INGREDIENTS:

- Shucked oysters - 12
- Unsalted butter - 1 lb.
- Chopped green onions - 1 bunch

- Honey Hog BBQ Rub or Meat Church "The Gospel" - 1 Tbsp.
- Minced green onions - 1/2 bunch
- Seasoned breadcrumbs - 1/2 cup
- Cloves of minced garlic - 2
- Shredded pepper jack cheese - 8 ounce
- Trigger Heat and Sweet BBQ sauce

DIRECTIONS:

1. Preheat the pellet grill for about 10-15 minutes with the lid closed.
2. To make the compound butter, wait for the butter to soften. Then combine the butter, onions, BBQ rub, and garlic thoroughly.
3. Lay the butter evenly on plastic wrap or parchment paper. Roll it up in a log shape and tie the ends with butcher's twine. Place these in the freezer to solidify for an hour. This butter can be used on any kind of grilled meat to enhance its flavor. Any other high-quality butter can also replace this compound butter.
4. Shuck the oysters, keeping the juice in the shell.
5. Sprinkle all the oysters with breadcrumbs and place them directly on the grill. Allow them to cook for 5 minutes. You will know they're cooked when the oysters begin to curl slightly at the edges.
6. Once they are cooked, put a spoonful of the compound butter on the oysters. Once the butter melts, you can add a little bit of pepper jack cheese to add more flavor to them.

7. The oysters must not be on the grill for longer than 6 minutes, or you risk overcooking them. Put a generous squirt of the BBQ sauce on all the oysters. Also, add a few chopped onions.
8. Let it cool and enjoy the taste of the sea!

NUTRITION: Carbohydrates: 2.5 g Protein: 4.7 g Fat: 1.1 g Sodium: 53 mg Cholesterol: 25 mg

Grilled Shrimp

Preparation time: 5 minutes

Cooking time: 4 minutes

Servings: 4

Preferred Wood Pellet: Oak or Alder

INGREDIENTS:

- Jumbo shrimp peeled and cleaned - 1 lb.
- Oil - 2 Tbsp.
- Salt - 1/2 Tbsp.
- Skewers - 4-5

- Pepper – 1/8 Tbsp.
- Garlic salt - 1/2 Tbsp.

DIRECTIONS:

1. Preheat the wood pellet grill to 375 degrees.
2. Mix all the ingredients in a small bowl.
3. After washing and drying the shrimp, mix it well with the oil and seasonings.
4. Add skewers to the shrimp and set the bowl of shrimp aside.
5. Open the skewers and flip them.
6. Cook for 4 more minutes. Remove when the shrimp is opaque and pink.

NUTRITION: Carbohydrates: 1.3 g Protein: 19 g Fat: 1.4 g Sodium: 805 mg Cholesterol: 179 mg

Teriyaki Smoked Shrimp

Preparation time: 5 minutes

Cooking time: 12 minutes

Servings: 6

Preferred Wood Pellet: Oak or Alder

INGREDIENTS:

- Uncooked shrimp - 1 lb.
- Onion powder - 1/2 Tbsp.
- Garlic powder - 1/2 Tbsp.
- Teriyaki sauce - 4 Tbsp.
- Mayo - 4 Tbsp.
- Minced green onion - 2 Tbsp.
- Salt - 1/2 Tbsp.

DIRECTIONS:

1. Remove the shells from the shrimp and wash thoroughly.
2. Preheat the wood pellet grill to 450 degrees.
3. Put with garlic powder, onion powder, and salt.
4. Cook the shrimp for 5-6 minutes on each side.
5. Take off the shrimp from the grill and garnish it with spring onion, teriyaki sauce, and mayo.

NUTRITION: Carbohydrates: 2 g Protein: 16 g Sodium: 1241 mg Cholesterol: 190 mg

Measurement Conversion Chart

Volume Equivalents (Liquid)

US STANDARD	US STANDARD (OUNCES)	METRIC (APPROXIMATE)
2 tablespoons	1 fl. ounce.	30 ml
1/4 cup	2 fl. ounce.	60 ml
1/2 cup	4 fl. ounce.	120 ml
1 cup	8 fl. ounce.	240 ml
11/2 cups	12 fl. ounce.	355 ml
2 cups or 1 pint	16 fl. ounce.	475 ml
4 cups or 1 quart	32 fl. ounce.	1 l
1 gallon	128 fl. ounce.	4 l

Volume Equivalents (Dry)

US STANDARD	METRIC (APPROXIMATE)
1/4 teaspoon	1 ml
1/2 teaspoon	2 ml
1 teaspoon	5 ml
1 tablespoon	15 ml
1/4 cup	59 ml
cup	79 ml
1/2 cup	118 ml
1 cup	177 ml

Oven Temperatures

FAHRENHEIT (F)	CELSIUS (C) (APPROXIMATE)
250°F	120 °C
300°F	150°C
325°F	165°C
350°F	180°C
375°F	190°C
400°F	200°C

425°F	220°C
450°F	230°C

Weight Equivalents

US STANDARD	METRIC (APPROXIMATE)
1/2 ounce	15 g
1 ounce	30 g
2 ounces	60 g
4 ounces	115 g
8 ounces	225 g
12 ounces	340 g
16 ounces or 1 pound	455 g

CPSIA information can be obtained
at www.ICGtesting.com
Printed in the USA
BVHW041338090621
609196BV00002B/3